LET'S WALK THERE!

Series Editor: Bruce Bedford

Southern Scotland

Atholl Innes

Line drawings by William Lees

JAVELIN BOOKS

POOLE · NEW YORK · SYDNEY

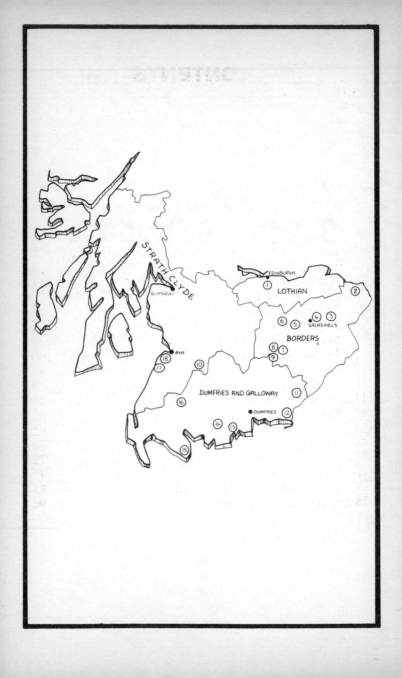

CONTENTS

First published in the UK 1987 by Javelin Books,
Link House, West Street, Poole, Dorset, BH15 1LL

Copyright © 1987 Javelin Books

Distributed in Australia by
Capricorn Link (Australia) Pty Ltd,
PO Box 665, Lane Cove, NSW 2066

British Library Cataloguing in Publication Data

Innes, Atholl
    Southern Scotland — (Let's Walk There!)
    1. Walking — Scotland — Guide-books
    2. Scotland — Description and travel —
    1981 — Guide-books
    I. Title   II. Series
    914.13′04858   DA870

ISBN 0 7137 1768 8

Cartography by Ron Rigby

Cover picture:
Neidpath Castle courtesy of Eric Anderson Photographer,
The Studio, Melrose, Roxburghshire

Typeset by Inforum Ltd, Portsmouth
Printed in Great Britain by
Cox & Wyman Ltd, Reading, Berks

INTRODUCTION

As worthwhile as any walk might be, it becomes doubly appealing if it takes you to some place of special interest. The nine books in this series, covering England, Scotland and Wales were conceived to describe just such walks.

A full description of the walk's objective is given at the start of each chapter. The objectives are diverse, giving a wide choice. Most are non-seasonal, and involve little walking in themselves once you are there.

Following the description of the objective, each section of the walk is clearly described, and a specially drawn map makes route-finding straightforward. As well as detailing the route, the authors describe many subsidiary points of interest encountered along the way.

The walks are varied and easy to follow. None of them is too taxing, except in the severest weather. Most are circular, returning you to your car at the starting point. Family walkers with young children will find plenty of shorter routes to suit their particular needs, whilst those with longer legs can select from more substantial walks.

The routes have been carefully chosen to include only well-established routes, and readers will certainly increase the enjoyment which they and others derive from the countryside if they respect it by following the Country Code.

Bruce Bedford
Series Editor

Walk 1
ARTHUR'S SEAT
LOTHIAN
4 miles

Edinburgh, Scotland's capital city, has been called the Athens of the north – a city of many gems, and the jewel in Scotland's crown. It is famous for its castle, the Palace of Holyrood, the Royal Mile, Princes Street, and the Calton Hill.

Yet, set in the middle of this city of almost half a million people are additional fine attractions for the walker: many acres of open parkland, such as Holyrood Park – a rich area of pastureland and green dominated by the volcanic rock of Arthur's Seat. It is on this ancient foundation that the city is built, and from many parts of the city as well as the high hills of the Borders and Fife the rock can be seen as the dominating feature of this festival city.

There is so much else for the visitor to see in Edinburgh that Arthur's Seat might easily be neglected. Yet the rock looms over Holyrood Palace, like some majestic guardian, defending the residence of the Queen while she is in the city. The parkland takes the explorer away from the continuous throbbing of traffic to a quiet country within a city.

The walk begins at Duddingston Loch, a bird sanctuary and nature reserve where there are varied interesting species of duck and geese. It adjoins Duddingston village, with its twelfth-century church. The area is well served by Lothian Regional Council public bus services and details of all local services are obtainable from their headquarters in the city's Queen Street.

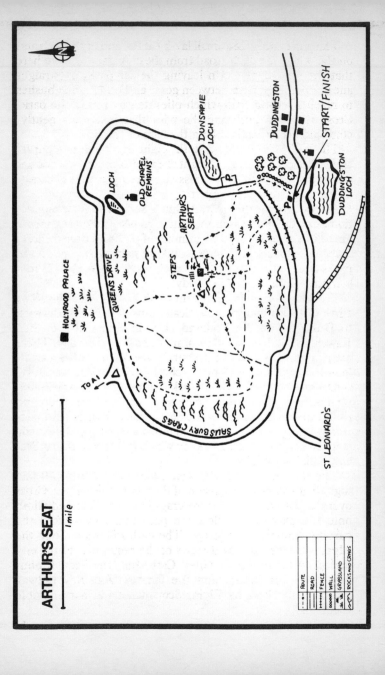

ARTHUR'S SEAT

1 mile

+—+—+	ROUTE
	ROAD
+++++	FENCE
□□□□	WALL
₩₩	GRASSLAND
∽∽	ROCKS AND CRAGS

START/FINISH

DUDDINGSTON

DUNSAPIE LOCH

DUDDINGSTON LOCH

LOCH

OLD CHAPEL REMAINS

ARTHUR'S SEAT

STEPS

HOLYROOD PALACE

QUEENS DRIVE

TO A1

SALISBURY CRAGS

ST LEONARD'S

There is parking in a small lay-by at the end of the loch and on the other side of the road from the church; it is from here that the walk begins. On leaving the car park, go straight ahead up a steep path between gorse and other small bushes to reach a second road which plies its way round the park. Cross the road and take the path that meanders gently, climbing occasionally, along the side of the hill.

The path swings round to the right in a moderate curve, and you should then go straight ahead. Volcanic rock dominates to the right while the grass-strewn slopes offer contrasting monochromes to the left.

As you go over the crest, Arthur's Seat, with its triangulation point and viewpoint indicator, comes into view approximately 300 yards ahead. A number of paths criss-cross here; make straight for the summit, taking particular care on the paths which climb through the rocky outcrops to the 823 foot summit. Hold on if it is windy.

From the top the magnificent views are breathtaking. The Firth of Forth sweeps majestically down via North Berwick to Dunbar, and the Lomond Hills in Fife and even Ben Lawers in Perthshire can be pinpointed on a clear day. There are panoramic views of Edinburgh, seemingly only an arm's length away; for that alone the climb is well worth the effort.

Descend to the foot of the rocky summit by the same route, turn left, and follow the track in an easterly direction and round the eastern flank of the Seat, where another path rises from Dunsapie Loch. Go ahead down a set of specially made steps to reach the narrow valley which dissects Arthur's Seat and Salisbury Crags.

The tops of Salisbury Crags, a face of rock over 60 feet high, brings a new dimension of the city to the walker. Cross over the path that divides the crags from the Seat and climb onto the plateau to follow the path that leads round the curving summit of the crags. The path follows close to the edge, and there are good views of the remainder of the city including the castle, St Giles' Cathedral, the Scott Monument, Princes Street, and the famous Waverley railway station from where the Flying Scotsman made many notable excursions.

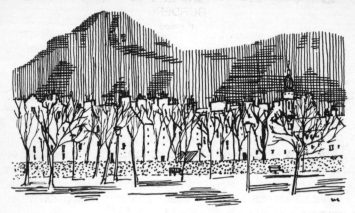

Arthur's Seat, with its panoramic views of Edinburgh

It is pleasant walking on the crags: gentle, rolling, and descending slowly. On the right, on the west face of the Seat, a narrow cleft of rock, not unlike a house chimney, tapers out into whin and scree, and finally grass. One can descend by this route, but it is not recommended.

Once again cross the path that runs through the valley, but do not go as far as the small lochan, over which stand the stone remains of an old chapel. Follow the path to the right, climbing easily between rocks to the foot of the Seat. Turn left onto the path and steps descended earlier in the walk.

Climb to the top of the steps and then take the path that doubles back and goes round in a horseshoe curve to reach the loch of Dunsapie. At the road turn right and pass a lay-by to where a fence begins on the left.

A number of steps leads down from here to grassland and then a large wall. Turn right and descend on the path to the road at Duddingston Loch, helped by a series of steps. Turn right to reach the car park just beyond a cottage.

Walk 2
ST ABBS WILDLIFE RESERVE
BORDERS
6 miles

St Abbs Wildlife and Nature Reserve is perched on one of the most rugged and precipitous stretches of coastline on the entire east coast of Scotland. It juts out sharply and pointedly, and in rough conditions its sheer cliffs are buffetted by the roaring North Sea almost 300 feet below.

Under joint management of the National Trust for Scotland, who bought it in 1980, and the Scottish Wildlife Trust, the reserve comprises a total of 192 acres of both cliffs and coastal headland, piercing out into the North Sea. The harbour of St Abbs nestles in the shelter of the volcanic rock that dominates the coastline.

The reserve is famous as a breeding ground for a wide variety of seabirds, with kittiwakes, razorbills, fulmars and guillemots flitting in and out of the rock and shoreline. On land, stonechats and wheatears are very much in evidence.

At the west end of the reserve stands St Abbs lighthouse, warning shipping of the dangers of sailing too close to the coastline. The reserve also has a ranger, and it is recommended that large parties in particular should make contact before setting out into the reserve.

St Abbs is served by a bus service from Berwick-upon-Tweed which also passes through Eyemouth and Coldingham. Buses also operate between Edinburgh and Berwick and pass through Coldingham, where the walk begins. It is possible to shorten the walk by about 3¼ miles by starting at the parking and information area at Northfield Farm.

ST ABB'S WILDLIFE RESERVE

1 mile

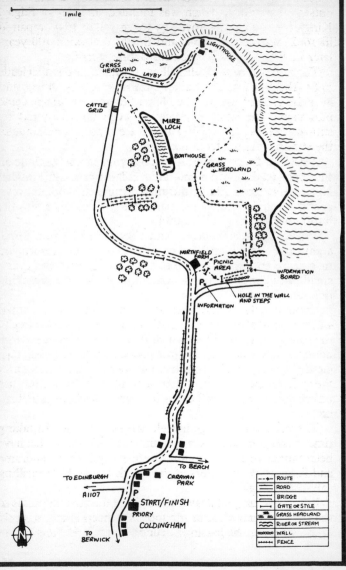

LIGHTHOUSE

GRASS HEADLAND

LAYBY

CATTLE GRID

MIRE LOCH

BOATHOUSE

GRASS HEADLAND

NORTHFIELD FARM

PICNIC AREA

P

INFORMATION BOARD

HOLE IN THE WALL AND STEPS

INFORMATION

TO BEACH

TO EDINBURGH

CARAVAN PARK

A1107

P

START/FINISH

PRIORY

COLDINGHAM

TO BERWICK

N

– · – ·	ROUTE
———	ROAD
⊞⊞⊞	BRIDGE
—⊔—	GATE or STILE
⋅⋅⋅⋅	GRASS HEADLAND
≈≈≈	RIVER or STREAM
▭▭▭	WALL
✛✛✛	FENCE

There are a number of parking areas in Coldingham (ten miles up the coast from Berwick), but the walk will begin outside the Priory, which was founded in 1098 by Edgar, King of the Scots, destroyed by Cromwell in 1648, repaired in 1662, restored in 1854, and finally renovated 100 years later in 1954. It is still used for public worship.

The first part of the walk follows the main road which leads to St Abbs, and as the walker climbs out of the village and over the crest of the hill the North Sea and the village come into view, the latter a peaceful haven and favoured by sub-aqua clubs. Its serenity and peace is indeed welcome to the summer visitor from the city.

A path leads down to St Abbs, but you should continue on the main road to a parking area and information kiosk at Northfield Farm. Here, the mixed ingredients of farming and inquisitive visitor have married and blossomed with the influx of naturalist and picnicker.

Marker posts direct you around the outskirts of the farm to a path running parallel to the road to St Abbs, before you turn sharp left at a high wall and then follow the path over a small bridge and through a number of gates before reaching the open headland.

Great care should be taken at all times, particularly if the wind is from the west, as the path on occasions passes close to the rocky coastline. The high cliffs, with their wildlife set in nature's true environment, present some of the most spectacular scenery in the country. On such a high promontory the air is always bracing both in summer and winter. It is not unknown for the whin bushes to be in full bloom in February.

The path at this stage is well defined. It is worth taking time to halt, perhaps taking advantage of a few seats that have been suitably placed, to admire the magnificent panorama and listen to the breakers of the North Sea and the thrilling call of the wildlife.

For a time the path leaves the sight of the sea and passes to the west of Kirk Hill; in the foothills sheep graze, scarcely acknowledging the passing intruder. But it is not long before

St Abbs Lighthouse, viewed from the Wildlife Reserve

the sea comes into view again, and the lighthouse. This is private property, and you must pass round the west of the buildings to reach the road, which leads down to Northfield.

Straight ahead, the ocean batters the coast for mile upon mile. Follow the road's twisting route downhill, to reach a cosy inlet at Pettico Wick, with a slipway perhaps holding stories of days of smuggling, now used by divers.

Turn left here – there is no evidence of a distinct track – before reaching a part of the road where it begins to climb and there is a cattle grid. On the left is Mire Loch, a narrow, neat passage of water which boasts numerous wildlife. Cross over a stile and follow a path down the right-hand side of the loch. The path will guide the walker through shrubland and trees, some planted in the memory of a Peter Howard Forster, who, a plaque tells us, 'loved this headland but who was lost in a diving accident in 1981.'

At the end of Mire Loch, which was dammed in 1901, is a boathouse, camouflaged in the trees, its tiled roof showing signs of strain from the strength of the wind that often batters the coast.

At the end of the loch, a track leads uphill to the right, passing a small thicket of trees and through two gates to rejoin the road which began at the lighthouse. On joining the road, turn left and continue on it to reach the cluster of cottages and farm at Northfield. From there, follow the road back to Coldingham.

Walk 3
SMAILHOLM TOWER
BORDERS
5 miles

A motorist on the road from Galashiels to the village of Smailholm in Roxburghshire has a striking view of Smailholm Tower on its lofty perch overlooking the moss of Bemersyde. The 57 foot-high tower is set on a rocky base at a gathering of old roads in the Mertoun parish, commanding a view of the network of ditches that drain Whitrig bog. Smailholm Tower, which is under the care and protection of the Ancient Monuments Division of the Scottish Development Department, is open to visitors from March to September.

The area around Smailholm has historical links back to the twelfth century, and it is known that monks from Dryburgh Abbey received land in 1160 on which they grazed sheep. They also owned, or had control of, a hospital and a corn mill. The painter, Turner, visited Smailholm in 1831 and sketched views of the tower and the lands surrounding it.

In 1799 the tower was almost razed to the ground and was saved only by the intervention of the writer Sir Walter Scott whose home was at Abbotsford, near Melrose. Sir Walter appealed to the owner, Scott of Harden, to retain the tower for he had spent much of his childhood at Sandyknowe, with his grandparents. Scott of Harden listened carefully to Sir Walter, and they struck a deal. The outcome was that Sir Walter agreed to write a ballad about Smailholm, and this he duly accomplished. 'The Eve of Saint John' was the result, a story of murder intermingled with romance. Scott went one

SMAILHOLM TOWER

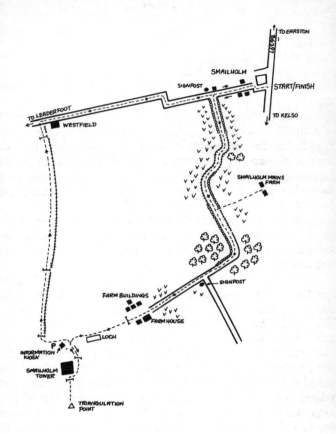

1 mile

To EARSTON
B6397

SMAILHOLM

SIGNPOST

START/FINISH

TO LEADERFOOT

TO KELSO

WESTFIELD

SMAILHOLM MAINS
FARM

FARM BUILDINGS

SIGNPOST

FARM HOUSE

LOCH

INFORMATION
KIOSK

SMAILHOLM
TOWER

TRIANGULATION
POINT

· - · →	ROUTE
═══	ROAD
⊃⊂	BRIDGE
├──┤	GATE OR STILE
∞∞∞	WALL
+++++	FENCE
ᵛ ᵛ ᵛᵥ	PASTURE

better when he mentioned Smailholm in *Marmion*, one of the Waverley novels.

The tower stands 57 feet high. Its walls are said to be seven feet thick and it has five storeys. According to James Reed's *The Border Ballads*, the 'parapet walk had a watchman's seat with a recess for a lantern.' It looks across to a neighbouring tower, Hume Castle, now roofless.

Around Smailholm the country is flat and arable, with the River Tweed meandering its way to the North Sea at Berwick-upon-Tweed. But from the tower there are commanding views of the pastoral Border countryside, with, in the distance to the south, Muckle Cheviot, that dominating peak that provides a barrier between England and Scotland. In summer it is often coated in mist; in winter it wears a mantle of snow.

The walk begins at the village of Smailholm, a cluster of cottages with a Post Office, set in the heart of farmland. It is served by public bus services from Kelso.

There are ample parking areas in and around the village. Begin the walk at the village hall, near which there is a signpost pointing the way up a road to the tower. Turn up this road, quiet and narrow, the hedgerows and walls neat and tidy. Ignore the narrow track leading off to the left to Smailholm Mains farm, and continue to the next junction, just past a short stretch of woodland. Here, another signpost points the way straight ahead to Smailholm Tower.

The road is now straight until you reach Sandyknowe Farm where the track dissects the farmhouse and the remainder of the farm. Take the track that goes slightly to the right, through a gate, and after about 100 yards the tower will come into full view. On the left is a small lochan, and whin bushes and rocky outcrops mark a change in landscape.

At the end of the track there is parking and an information kiosk which will provide visitors with all they want to know about Smailholm. From here, a track leads to the tower; in wet weather the rocks will be very slippery. The entrance to the tower is reached through a gate and the doorway faces west, giving welcome shelter if the wind is out of the east.

Smailholm Tower, scene of happy childhood days for Sir Walter Scott

The walk can be extended slightly by taking the exit to the north of the tower and crossing some open land to the triangulation point, next to a disused building, lying at a height of 679 feet.

Retrace your steps back to the tower and return to the information kiosk before turning left then right to follow an old farm road, passing through three sets of gates to reach the road at the white cottages of Westfield. Turn right and follow the road for one and a half miles to return to Smailholm village.

Walk 4
MELROSE ABBEY
BORDERS

4 miles

Melrose Abbey, one of the finest in Scotland, is the focal point of this walk that will take the walker along the banks of the River Tweed.

The abbey was founded in 1136 by monks from the Cistercian abbey of Rievaulx in Yorkshire. During the years it has suffered mercilessly at the hands of English raiders. Melrose is one of the most historical and beautiful abbeys in Scotland, and is one of four in the Borders, the others being Dryburgh, Jedburgh, and Kelso. Together they bring a rich culture to an area steeped in history.

The abbey suffered badly during the invasion of Richard II in 1385 and was rebuilt. Following another invasion, this time by the Earl of Hertford, the ruins became a stone quarry for local people. The year 1986 was a significant one for the abbey when its 850th anniversary was celebrated with a number of events in the abbey and in Melrose. The abbey is the resting place of the heart of King Robert the Bruce, and all this history comes alive again each June when a number of ceremonies connected with the Melrose Festival take place among the ruins. Large crowds will gather to witness the installation of the Melrosian and the Melrose Festival Queen – a ceremony of majesty and pageantry in a beautiful setting under the mantle of the Eildon Hills.

Melrose, with a population of around 2,000, is a tourist-orientated centre with the abbey only one of a number of attractions for visitors. It is served by public bus transport

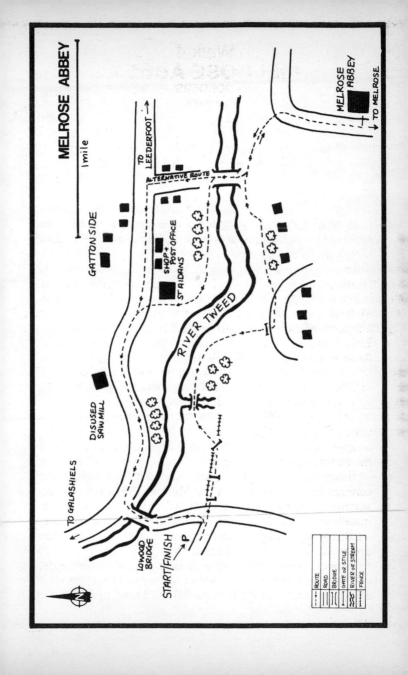

from Galashiels, St Boswells, and Jedburgh.

The walk begins near the road bridge of Lowood, adjacent to the road leading from Galashiels to Leaderfoot. Parking is on the west side of the bridge on an area of land at the entrance to a garden centre. To start, cross the road, climb the stile, and follow the path down to the banks of the River Tweed. The path is part of the Southern Upland Way, the long-distance footpath from Portpatrick by the Irish Sea to Cockburnspath by the North Sea. It was opened in 1984 by Michael Ancram, Minister of State at the Scottish Office in Edinburgh.

Two other stiles are crossed before you enter pleasant meadowland; Mallard ducks and swans frequent the river while the trees resound to the call of the birds. As the path follows the curve of the river, you will see on the right the rear of the Waverley Castle, one of several hotels in the Melrose district.

As you approach Melrose, the river cuts in sharply and you are forced onto a 25 yard stretch of road before joining a wider cinder track high above the river, with houses perched on the right. Here there are magnificent views across to the carefully conserved village of Gattonside, whose residents have fought to preserve its identity over the years.

Now you pass through some open parkland – there are a few seats for those who wish to take a break in comfort before again descending to the banks of the river and crossing a small stream to reach the feature known locally as the Chain Bridge, its cantilevers spanning the Tweed at a wide part of the river.

To reach the abbey, go straight ahead until you reach the A6091 road from Leaderfoot to Melrose. Follow this to the right until the abbey is reached, on the left.

After visiting the abbey, return to the Chain Bridge. One of the first suspension bridges in Scotland, it was opened in October 1826. No more than eight people should be on it at one time, and remember that it is an offence to make the bridge rock or swing!

There is a superb view of the Eildon Hills, well worth a

Melrose Abbey, founded in 1136

walk on their own. The North Eildon was the site of an Iron Age hill fort which held a position of strength in its commanding site.

Having crossed the bridge, the walker can either continue into the village of Gattonside and turn left at the main road or turn left at the end of the bridge and follow the track past Melrose Cauld, a fast stretch of water made by the abbey monks to take water to their mill lake. Whichever route is chosen, the paths meet at the entrance to St Aidan's, a home for the mentally handicapped.

Follow then the footpath leading past a disused sawmill, on the right, to reach Lowood Bridge. Your starting point is on the opposite side of the bridge.

Walk 5
TRAQUAIR HOUSE
BORDERS
5 miles

Traquair House is distinguished as being the oldest inhabited house in Scotland. Yet it is much more than that; one of the biggest tourist attractions in the south of Scotland, it draws more than 60,000 visitors through its doors every year. Aspects of its turbulent history have been integrated with a number of attractions – craft workshops, an annual fair, a brewery, a maze, and garden walks.

Traquair House is also famous for the Bear Gates which stand closed at the end of the tree-lined avenue leading from the house. The gates were closed one autumn day in 1745 by the fifth Earl; he had just wished his famous guest, Prince Charles Edward Stuart, a safe journey with the promise that the gates would not be reopened until the Stuarts were restored to the throne. They remain shut to this day.

It is claimed that the house goes back to the year 950, but it is known for certain that in 1107 Alexander I stayed there and granted a charter to Traquair. Since the twelfth century no fewer than 27 Scottish and English monarchs have stayed there. The house has changed little in appearance since the seventeenth century.

Mary Queen of Scots was one of Traquair's notable visitors, and on display in the house are her rosary, crucifix, purse, the cradle in which she nursed her son and future king of Scotland and England, James VI, and the armorial in oak with the queen's cipher marking her visit to Traquair in 1566.

TRAQUAIR HOUSE

1 mile

START/FINISH

INNERLEITHEN
HALL ST
P
FACTORY
TO GALASHIELS

DIRECTIONAL SIGN

TO PEEBLES

HOTEL

GARAGE

CEMETERY

TWEED BRIDGE

RIVER TWEED

TO WALKERBURN

TO PEEBLES

POOL

TRAQUAIR HOUSE

CRAFT WORKSHOPS AND TEA ROOMS

LODGE

QUAIR WATER

PHONE KIOSK

HALL

MILL

DROVE ROAD TO MINCHMOOR

TRAQUAIR VILLAGE

SCHOOL

TO ST MARY'S LOCH

N

- - + -	ROUTE
═══	ROAD
▦	BRIDGE
≋≋	RIVER OR STREAM

The name Traquair comes from Tra, meaning a dwelling or hamlet, and the Quair – the tributary of the River Tweed which runs behind the house – means a stream with a winding course.

The walk begins two miles from Traquair in the decidedly quaint town of Innerleithen, a community steeped in Border history and folklore. The town retains its own identity and independence to mark its stature as distinct from its county town of Peebles. The Pirn Hill and Caerlee Hill forts dominate the town which, though seemingly sandwiched, provides the focal point for main arterial roads to Galashiels, Peebles, and the Yarrow Valley.

The first recorded reference to the town dates to the reign of Malcolm IV in the twelfth century when the ancient parish church was given by the monarch to the monks of Kelso. The town is famous for St Ronan's Well, and during the festival celebrations in July the Standard Bearer – the young man chosen to represent the Burgh – drinks from the medicinal waters of the well.

The town lies on the A72, between Peebles and Galashiels. Parking is available in Hall Street, which leads to the town's Victoria Park. The house is open from March to October. A bus service linking Galashiels and Peebles passes through the town.

Begin at the west end of the main street. There is a considerable amount of road walking, but fortunately the country roads are quiet. Cross the A72 road and follow the Traquair Road past a hotel on the left. A long stretch of roadway brings you to the bridge spanning the River Tweed, and it is not unknown after heavy rain for the river to rise so much that it actually touches or even laps over onto the roadway.

After a further 300 yards, the road curves to the right, and before long the lodge house is reached on the right from where a path leads to Traquair House. This is also an exit for motor traffic. Purchase your ticket for entry to the grounds and house at a kiosk on the main driveway leading to the house.

Traquair House, the oldest inhabited house in Scotland

Having visited the house and grounds, make your exit via the entrance, and on reaching the roadway turn left. 200 yards along there is a hump-backed bridge, from where the right-hand fork should be taken past the mill to reach the road leading over to St Mary's Loch.

Turn left on this road for Fingland Bridge, and continue following it to the village of Traquair. Here, the Southern Upland Way – the long-distance footpath from Portpatrick to Cockburnspath – rises on the right and follows the old drove road over to Yarrowford. This famous route crosses Minch Moor, and on the climb to the summit the hardened walker will pass the Cheese Well. Here, an offering of cheese will placate the fairies and ensure the traveller a safe journey.

However, there will be time only to imagine the difficulties of such a journey in days of old before you follow the road back to Innerleithen.

Walk 6
NEIDPATH CASTLE
BORDERS

5¾ miles

Neidpath Castle, an ancient fortress with a commanding view of the silvery River Tweed one mile west of the Royal Burgh of Peebles, is an outstanding example of a border pele tower. The L-shaped building has been inhabited since the early fourteenth century to the present day. During 1645 the castle was garrisoned against the Marquis of Montrose and in 1650 against the force of Cromwell.

The castle originally belonged to the Hay family, but in 1810 the estate passed to the Earls of Wemyss, and the building is now open to the public under the Wemyss and March Estates.

The castle plays a significant role in the Beltane Festival, an annual event to celebrate the Riding of the Marches, revived in 1897 to commemorate Queen Victoria's Diamond Jubilee. One of the most poignant ceremonies of the week-long celebrations is the installation of the Warden of Neidpath, a ceremony that goes back to 1930. The warden, from the steps of this ancient keep, then addresses the public; among notable persons to have filled this high position are MP David Steel and Lord Lieutenant Col Aidan M. Sprot.

The castle is open from Easter to October.

The walk begins in Peebles, the name of which is derived from the ancient word pebylls (tents) which were pitched there by the wandering Gadeni tribe, the founders of the town. Peebles is served by buses from Edinburgh, Galashiels, and Biggar. The start of the walk is a small car

31

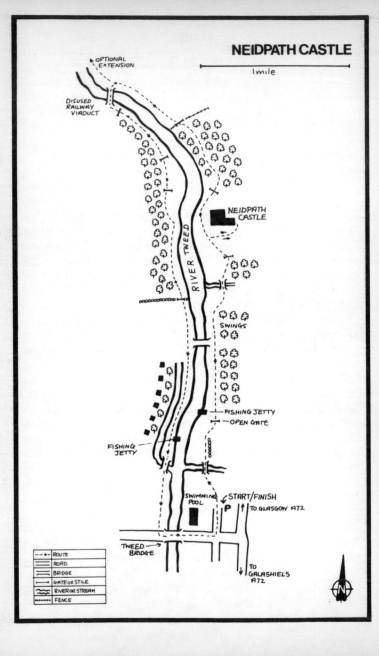

park adjacent to the swimming pool at the west end of the High Street.

As you leave the car park, the River Tweed, meandering gracefully and peacefully through the town, is on the left. A wooden bridge over Eddleston Water, known locally as the Cuddy, is crossed, and there is then a distinct path close to the river. The Hay Lodge Hospital complex is on the right as you enter Hay Lodge Park, a delightful area of ground and parkland, the home of Peebles rugby club. The park is set in beautiful surroundings with huge oak trees gracing the landscape; with the river famous for anglers, a fishing jetty has been built by Borders Regional Council's Community Programme for disabled fishermen.

Beyond Fotheringham Bridge, which gives the pedestrian a link with the opposite side of the river, the path curves round past a play area to enter a wooded section; here the walking is much rougher until a stile is reached. Beyond, the path cuts down to a wide grassy plain and Neidpath Castle comes into view high up on the right. On the approach to the castle, a narrow path leads up to the entrance gates.

After your visit, return to the path at the riverside and contour round the rocky promontory of the castle, over a stile, and along a wide, winding path through woodland before another stile, leading into a field, is reached. Straight ahead is the famous railway viaduct which carried the former Caledonian railway from Peebles to Symington. It is said that the architect carved his rough model from a turnip.

The main walk now crosses the river by this bridge. However, you can choose to continue another half a mile upstream and cross by the road bridge leading to the head of the impressive and appealing Manor Valley. Having crossed this road bridge, take the first fork on the left over the old Manor bridge, built in 1703; and go up the steep hill, taking time to cast a look back to some of the highest peaks in the Borders, including Dollar Law. A path leads into the woods on the left at the top of the hill, and this can be followed back into Peebles.

However, the main route will cross the earlier railway

Neidpath Castle, a perfect example of a Border pele tower

viaduct. As you cross you will see, straight ahead, the
boarded-up entrance to the South Park tunnel, which runs
almost three-quarters of a mile through the hill. Gangs of
Irish labourers built the tunnel in 1863.

On the far side of the viaduct, cross a stile on the left and
follow the path downhill to the bank of the river. There are
numerous paths, but it is advisable to follow the one closest to
the river. The path is rocky in parts and care will need to be
taken, particularly in wet weather. A fine view of the castle
can be obtained from Artist's Rock, situated at a part of the
river known as Gardenfoot. There is much evidence in the
castle of the damage caused by Cromwell's cannons which
bombarded the fortress from a high point on this side of the
river.

At the end of the wood, noted for its wildlife, the path
emerges via a stile into a tarmacadam track which leads back
to Peebles. The steeple of the old parish church is dominant

in the distance but on the right there is now no evidence of the former Caledonian railway station. Peebles at one time had two stations, linked by a loop line, the North British serving the line from Galashiels to Edinburgh.

The river slows, deeper as it approaches the Cauld via a stretch of water known as the Minnie. At the end of the path, turn left onto the road to cross the main Tweed Bridge, originally timber-built and stoneclad. Turn left again at the end of the bridge then descend to the car park.

Walk 7
ST MARY'S LOCH AND CHURCHYARD
BORDERS
8 miles

Unlike the Highlands, the south-east corner of Scotland is not endowed with many lochs, but St Mary's Loch, 16 miles from Selkirk on the A708 road to Moffat, is one of the most scenic stretches of water in the whole of the country.

Overlooking the loch from a hillside to the north-west is the ancient churchyard of St Mary's of the Lowes, a place of worship until the middle of the seventeenth century.

Several of the headstones have fallen over, but one can sense the history and the atmosphere of this historic place. Although there is no church, a service is held there each year in July. Called the Blanket Preaching, it brings a poignant moment in Border history home to those who have to perhaps brave the elements of wind and rain, even in the middle of summer.

The custom of the Blanket Preaching was started in the late nineteenth century by the Rev Dr James Russell. The name of Blanket Preaching is taken from the fact that a tent made from a blanket erected over a temporary framework of wood was used to protect the preacher from the weather.

This is an area steeped in prose, poetry and history, a land made famous by such writers as Sir Walter Scott and James Hogg, the Ettrick shepherd, whose statue overlooks the loch at its western extremity. Hogg really came to prominence in 1985 when a festival commemorated the 150th anniversary of his death.

The walk begins at the southern end of the loch at Tibbie

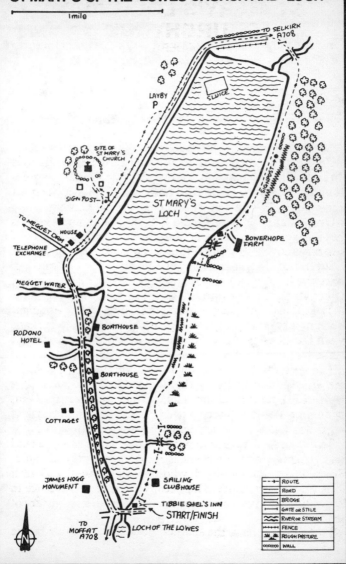

ST MARY'S OF THE LOWES CHURCH AND LOCH

1 mile

TO SELKIRK A708

LAYBY P

SLUICE

SITE OF ST MARY'S CHURCH

SIGN POST

ST MARY'S LOCH

SIGNPOST

TO MEGGET DAM

HOUSE

TELEPHONE EXCHANGE

BOWERHOPE FARM

MEGGET WATER

BOATHOUSE

RODONO HOTEL

BOATHOUSE

COTTAGES

JAMES HOGG MONUMENT

SAILING CLUBHOUSE

TIBBIE SHIEL'S INN
START/FINISH

TO MOFFAT A708

LOCH OF THE LOWES

N

--►--	ROUTE
≡≡≡	ROAD
⊏⊐	BRIDGE
⊢	GATE OR STILE
〜〜	RIVER OR STREAM
✚✚✚	FENCE
🌿🌿	ROUGH PASTURE
∞∞∞	WALL

Shiel's Inn, a hostelry noted over the years for its hospitality and warmth. Tibbie was the wife of a shepherd, and, when she died in 1878, she was aged 95.

The view from the inn looking down the loch is beautiful and breathtaking. It was here in 1984 that the Southern Upland Way, the long-distance footpath from Portpatrick to Cockburnspath, was opened, and there is a plaque on the wall of the inn to mark the occasion.

Due to the rural location, there is no public transport except on certain days during the summer months. There is, however, ample parking by the side of the Loch of the Lowes, a neighbour of St Mary's Loch.

The route will take you around the whole of the loch. Begin at the inn and pass by the clubhouse of St Mary's Loch Sailing Club. The loch is used for both sailing and fishing, and the waters are surrounded by high hills. On desolate winter days the waters can be whipped up into wild battalions of buffetting waves.

A number of stiles have been created along the route. You will soon reach a short thicket of wood, cross two stiles and a small wooden bridge, then go out into open pastureland on the lower slopes of Bowerhope Law.

Being part of a specific route, the path itself is well defined and time can be taken to watch the wildlife, including duck and swans, on the loch. Across the water is the small hamlet of Cappercleuch which once boasted a police station and a post office. It is now merely a cluster of cottages.

After just over a mile, pass through three gateways or cross over three stiles before going down to the edge of the loch near the farm of Bowerhope, the land of which in the fifteenth century was a forest standing. Once past the farm, cross a stile and join a wide track; this is the access road to Bowerhope. The track winds its way along the side of the loch with thick forest tucked in on the right-hand side.

At the end of the loch the track swings round towards Dryhope Farm, but at the junction with the main road, turn left, taking time to view, on the right behind the farm, the

St Mary's Church, scene of the annual Blanket Preaching

tower of Dryhope, birthplace of Mary Scott, the Flower of Yarrow.

You will soon be able to make use of a wide grassy verge on the right after reaching the western side of the loch. About 200 yards further on a signpost points the way to St Mary's churchyard. Climb the style and follow the path for just over a quarter of a mile to the old churchyard. A few seats have been placed beside the path, and finally a wooden bridge will bring the walker to the walled grounds.

To continue, descend the hillside to the road, turn right and follow it to Cappercleuch at the junction with the road leading to Tweedsmuir. This passes the Megget Dam, the objective of Walk 8 in this book. Continue on the Moffat road, passing over Megget Water, and then past the Rodono Hotel to reach the grassy slopes above Tibbie Shiel's Inn.

Walk 8
MEGGET RESERVOIR
BORDERS
4 miles

The Megget valley is long and wide, flanked by steeply rising hills, the tallest of which is Broad Law – at 2,756 feet, the highest south of Edinburgh on the eastern flank of Scotland. Hundreds of years ago, the valley was part of the Forest of Ettrick, a hunting land created by David I, and the country ran with deer for many centuries.

However, this century has witnessed a profound change of landscape. A 184-foot high dam has been built across the valley, stemming the flow of water to form the great tract of Megget reservoir, created to augment the water supply to Edinburgh. Megget valley was chosen as the best site because of its suitable profile, and the fact that it lies close to other reservoirs which serve the capital city. The reservoir, which was inaugurated in 1983, lies in the county of Ettrick and Lauderdale but comes under the auspices of the Lothian region.

The long-term effect on the valley of the creation of the reservoir has been immense. It was to change both the landscape and the old routes of communication of this farming community. No longer able to drive along the floor of the valley, motorists had to take to the new road – from Glengaber to Meggethead – built high above the reservoir. Farms were to disappear under the lapping waters, hidden forever. Before the reservoir was built, over a thousand sheep grazed in the valley. Now only stocked trout glide over the submerged terrain.

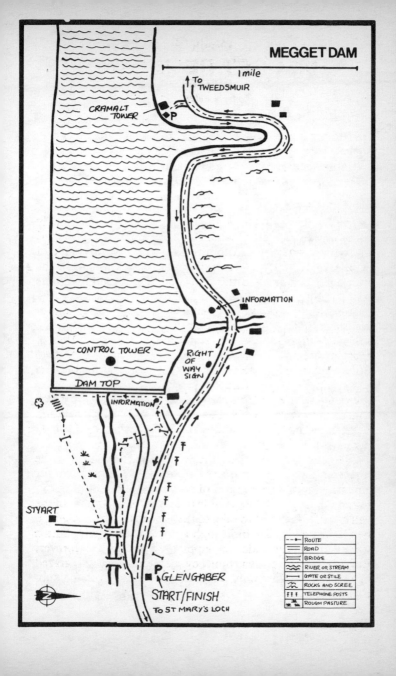

Despite all this, the valley has lost none of its traditional values. New steadings and houses have been built to replace those now drowned, and the new steadings certainly give improved facilities for the farmer and shepherd during the winter months and at lambing time. The planners and builders of the reservoir have successfully blended it into the environment, and it has added its own stamp of character to what was once a grey and desolate place – much of the improvement due to the planting of new trees and shrubs. The ancient towers of Cramalt were saved, and the remains rebuilt as one tower base with superlative views down towards St Mary's Loch.

The valley, not surprisingly, has a high average rainfall; it is equally spectacular in summer and winter, and in the coldest weather the water can freeze over. There are numerous parking places along the top of the dam, and information boards – colourful panels at various vantage points – give the history of the valley and the reservoir. Walkers are catered for by well signposted routes.

Though the area is not served by public transport, access is easy for the motorist. The reservoir lies by the minor road linking Tweedsmuir on the A701 and Cappercleuch (15 miles west of Selkirk) on the A708. Though there is parking on the dam top, this walk begins at Glengaber, a quarter of a mile east of the dam, so this is your parking place and starting point.

Start by following the road to the dam top and continue on the road, keeping the reservoir on the left. You will pass a Scottish Rights of Way Society sign pointing to the Manor Valley near Peebles, and then reach a parking area and information panels from where there are extensive views of the loch and the valley.

Steep-sided hills close in as the road winds its way westwards. Continue to Cramalt, a mile further on the road, at the end of a horseshoe curve round an intensive spur of the reservoir. Just beyond a cottage take the track that leads down to the side of the reservoir where there is a parking area and picnic tables. Here stand the remains of the ancient

Megget Dam, built to augment Edinburgh's water supply

Cramalt Tower, believed to have been four storeys high at one time.

Retrace your steps to the dam top car park, the return journey giving a new outlook on the reservoir. Across the great stretch of water is Shielhope, draped in trees, and further west the track that leads to Winterhopeburn.

When you reach the dam top, halt a while to learn more about the reservoir from the information panels. Then cross the high face of the dam to the opposite side of the valley to turn left and descend a few steps. Follow the track to a stile and then down through the field to reach another stile which leads onto a farm road. Turn left, cross the bridge, and then turn left again, following the sign marked 'footpaths'.

Go back along the bank of the overflow stream from the dam tower; cross to the right and over a stile to reach the road which leads into the chamber of the dam. It is possible to visit this chamber by prior arrangement with Lothian Regional Council.

Continue straight ahead over two stiles before turning left onto a track. On the right is an Ordnance Survey triangulation point. Follow the track to reach another stile, situated next to the dam top. Turn right and walk down back to the road to Glengaber, your starting point.

Walk 9
GREY MARE'S TAIL
DUMFRIES & GALLOWAY
7 miles

The Grey Mare's Tail is a spectacular torrent of water, wild in winter and placid in summer, that cascades down from the eerie Loch Skeen. It is easily accessible from the A708 road that links Moffat in Dumfries & Galloway with Selkirk in Ettrick and Lauderdale. From the road there is a footpath to the foot of the waterfall, which drops almost 300 feet in the course of the Tail Burn which flows into Moffat Water

The Tail is set in a perfect example of a hanging valley or corrie, gouged out during the ice age. It is visible from the road, but the top is the only part clearly in sight. It is necessary to walk up via one of the two footpaths to see the waterfall in its entirety. It is a very popular spot with visitors in both summer and winter. The narrow, breathtaking valley offers a number of spots for a picnic, and the National Trust has provided information panels which tell visitors not only the history of the Tail, but also of other Trust properties in Scotland. In winter the Tail can be particularly spectacular; frozen solid, it provides a fine challenge for climbers who tackle its sheer crystal flutings with ice hammers and crampons.

The land surrounding the waterfall is owned by the National Trust for Scotland, who purchased the total of 2,382 acres in 1962, including the Tail itself. The purchase was made possible through the Trust's Mountainous Country Fund and other donations.

The path to the left (west) of the Tail Burn goes only as far

GREY MARE'S TAIL

|———————| 1mile

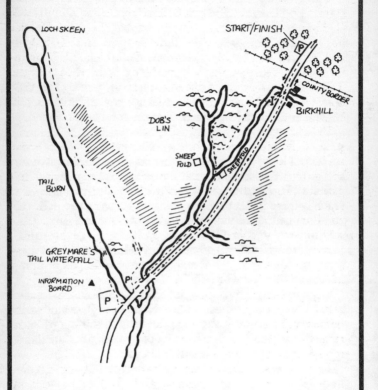

LOCH SKEEN

START/FINISH

P

COUNTY BORDER

BIRKHILL

DOB'S LIN

SHEEP FOLD

SHEEPFOLD

TAIL BURN

GREY MARE'S TAIL WATERFALL

INFORMATION BOARD

P

—·—·—	ROUTE
————	ROAD
=====	BRIDGE
——+——	GATE OR STILE
~~	RIVER OR STREAM
+++++	FENCE
~~	CRAGS
//////	HILLSIDE STEEP

as the foot of the waterfall. But our route takes the path on the right which climbs high above the Tail and continues on to Loch Skeen. This path has been eroded over the years and there have been a few accidents. Great caution should be exercised, particularly after rain.

The walk to the Tail begins near Birkhill, where the county boundaries of Ettrick & Lauderdale and Dumfries & Galloway meet. There is no public bus service, but a Harrier bus operates on certain days in the summer from Galashiels and Selkirk to Moffat. Telephone Galashiels 2237 for information. There is plenty of parking off the road near the Tail, but for this walk, drive to a small car park by the A708 next to a wood just north of Birkhill, over the border in Ettrick & Lauderdale. There is space for four or five cars.

On leaving the car park, turn right and follow the main road to the white cottage at Birkhill, lying 1,000 feet above sea level. Go through a gate on the right, cross a small stream, and go over farmland to reach another gate. Pass through this gate and, keeping the stream on the left, go straight ahead to reach a third gate. Go through and keep on the path that contours round the side of the hill to lead into a narrow and striking rocky gorge known as Dob's Lin – a geologist's paradise. Here the walker can enjoy solitude and calm away from the noise of traffic and secluded from most others making their way up to the Tail.

Continue through the gorge, crossing the stream if necessary to follow the best path, until the stream divides. It would be possible for those with experience to climb out onto the ridge by one of the two gorges, but for this walk, one should retrace steps to the foot of the valley.

Follow the stream as it meanders down, and where it goes under a road go straight ahead to reach the path that leads up the right of the Tail. There are steps at first, but then the path becomes a natural hill path offering superb views down to the Tail and into Moffatdale.

The path keeps to the right of the Tail burn to reach the lonely loch of Loch Skeen, standing at 1,700 feet under the shadow of the mighty White Coombe. The loch is well

Grey Mare's Tail, which is under the auspices of the National Trust for Scotland

patronised by anglers and is felt by many to be the most beautiful setting of any loch south of the Great Glen. Surrounded by hills, it presents an eerie setting, particularly when the mist is low and enshrouds the hills; and again, when wind funnelled up from the valley whips the water into roaring waves.

Turn round here and follow the path all the way down to the foot of the Tail. At the road, turn left and walk past Birkhill to reach the car park.

Walk 10
WANLOCKHEAD LEAD MUSEUM
STRATHCLYDE
6 miles

At an altitude of 1531 feet, Wanlockhead is the highest village in Scotland and at one time, along with neighbouring Leadhills, it was a thriving lead mining community. The area's importance depended on deposits of gold and silver as well as lead, and it is said that on one occasion a nugget of gold weighing five ounces was found at Wanlockhead.

Although lead mining ceased many years ago, the remains of the industry are still very much in evidence today. The Wanlockhead Museum Trust set up a museum in the village to relate with a high degree of realism the history of an industry which meant valuable jobs for this tiny Strathclyde community. It is also possible to travel undergound to visit one of the mines and experience the conditions under which the workers earned their living.

The route will take you from Leadhills over rough country to Wanlockhead, returning via the course of the former railway line, opened from Elvanfoot to Leadhills in 1901, and to Wanlockhead the following year, to carry lead from the mines to the central belt of Scotland. After the demise of the mines, the line closed eventually as well, but it had continued to be used by both freight and passenger traffic until 1938. However, at the time of writing there is a revival in railway preservation, and the Lowthers Railway Society have plans to reopen the line from Leadhills to Wanlockhead as a tourist attraction. A station building and engine shed are planned for Leadhills.

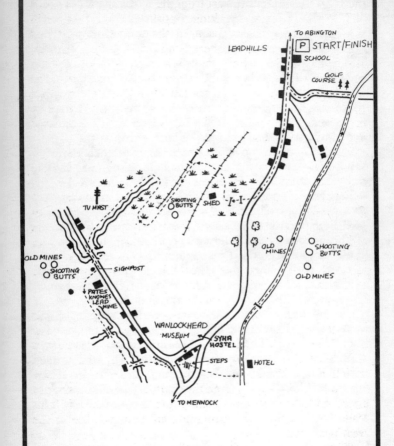

WANLOCKHEAD LEAD MUSEUM

TO ABINGTON

LEADHILLS

P START/FINISH

SCHOOL

GOLF COURSE

TV MAST

SHOOTING BUTTS

SHED

OLD MINES

SHOOTING BUTTS

OLD MINES

OLD MINES

SHOOTING BUTTS

SIGNPOST

PATES KNOWES LEAD MINE

WANLOCKHEAD MUSEUM

SYHA HOSTEL

STEPS

HOTEL

TO MENNOCK

	ROUTE
	ROAD
	BRIDGE
	GATE OR STILE
	RIVER OR STREAM
	FENCE
	GRASS OR HEATHER

N

This walk starts at the appropriately-named Leadhills. This village lies at the junction of three minor roads: the B797 and the B7040 (both leading south-west from the A74, and the B797 (leading north-east from the A76, nine miles north of Thornhill). There is parking opposite the police station in the main street and adjacent to the school. A post bus operates in the area, but there is no public transport to it.

Because of their height above sea-level, both villages can be subject to much wetter and colder weather than that of the valleys, and mist can often shroud the hills. If the weather forecast is bad, do not undertake this walk unless you are an experienced and well equipped hill walker with a large-scale map and a compass – and the ability to use both.

Leadhills is a quaint village – in the churchyard is the grave of John Taylor who died at the grand old age of 137. One can study the records of the lead mines in the local library.

From the car park, turn left and walk along the main street towards Wanlockhead. Leave the village, and shortly after passing the de-restriction signs take the path that leads to the right from the road. Follow this path through two sets of gates, set close together; pass a shed on your left and follow the path until a third gate is reached. Go through, and the path winds its way gently uphill to reach a fourth gate – don't go through this one.

Turn left here and follow the fence along the ridge, now at a height of almost 2,000 feet. This is rounded hill country with a base of grass and heather and stupendous views to the Lowther Hills. Continue through the heather along a track which is not always distinct, keeping close to the fence. Another fence comes in from the right, but continue straight ahead until the fence takes a sharp turn down to the left. This leads back to the road, providing an 'escape route' if the weather is foul.

Where the fence turns sharp left, cross over it and follow a narrow path to the edge of the ridge; far below will be seen the lead mines and a cemetery. Now fork right and join a path which swings round the head of the valley. Contour round to follow the ridge on the right of the valley, heading towards

Lochnell Mine, part of the lead museum complex

the old lead mines. You will soon reach a television mast; from here descend steeply to the road where it passes the cemetery.

Turn left to follow the road until a signpost indicating the Southern Upland Way, the long-distance footpath from Portpatrick to Cockburnspath, is reached. Turn right and follow the markers. On the left are the restored remains of part of the Pates Knowes smelt mill, which operated from 1764 to 1845. It has been excavated and conserved for the museum trust by a job creation team.

Continue to follow the markers of the Southern Upland Way to reach another indicator point which features a drawing by John Clerk of Eldin, in 1775, of the waterwheel pumping engine of the Strait Steps mine. Shortly on the left is the entrance to the Lochnell Mine, and tickets are obtainable from the museum for an escorted tour. Both mine and museum are open from Easter to September. Keep straight ahead to reach the museum close to the road junction. There is a picnic table here, and one can sit alongside two old wagons that once carried the lead from the mines.

After visiting the museum, go up the steps on the Southern Upland Way, cross the road that leads to the Mennock Pass, and continue to the former railway station at Wanlockhead.

Turn left here onto the trackbed of the old railway and cross over the road that leads to the radar station on the Lowther Hills. Pass through a narrow, rocky cutting, and continue over a stile to reach a straight stretch of the old track that leads past mines on either side. Go past a large house on the left and then the site of the old station to enter a second cutting. This will bring you out at a road adjacent to the golf course.

Turn left and follow the road down into the village. At the main street fork right and walk along the road to the car park.

Walk 11
MALCOLM MONUMENT
DUMFRIES & GALLOWAY
5 miles

High above the village of Langholm in Eskdale, 20 miles from Carlisle, stands a monument; few people who drive on the A7 linking this Cumbrian city with Edinburgh probably know very much about it or the man it commemorates.

The Malcolm Monument is in memory of Sir John Malcolm, born in 1769. At the age of 13, at his own request, he was commissioned into the East India Company. It was a career he was to follow to a high level, eventually becoming Governor of Bombay, a post he held from 1827 to 1830.

The first stone in the monument was laid by Sir James Graham, Grand Master of the Cumberland Lodge of Free Masons, and on the day no less than a thousand spectators climbed the 1,165 feet high Whita Hill to witness the occasion.

From the monument on a clear day there are exciting views on both sides of the border: westwards towards the Lake District and the impressive hulk of Skiddaw, and northwards through Eskdalemuir and round to the Hawick hills.

The walk, which begins in Langholm, the 'Muckle Toon', takes you to the monument as well as round some of this woollen mill town's famous sites. The first mill was built in 1750, and today the town is famous for its tweed, its Common Riding festival, and, of course, its rugby.

A regular bus service operates to Carlisle while there are through services between Carlisle and Edinburgh, linking with British Rail services at Carlisle.

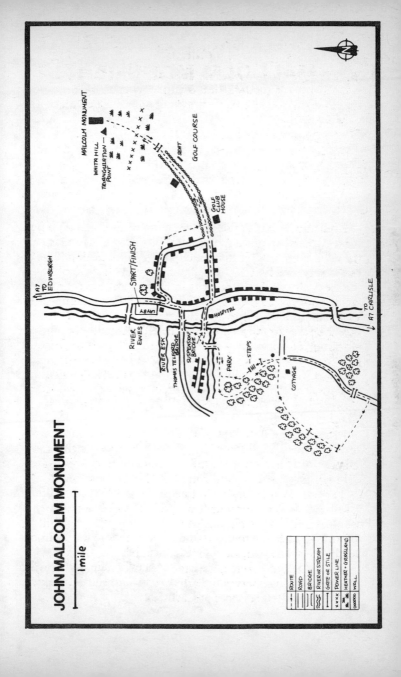

JOHN MALCOLM MONUMENT

1 mile

MALCOLM MONUMENT

WHITA HILL
TRIANGULATION —
POINT

GOLF COURSE

SEAT

GOLF
CLUB
HOUSE

START/FINISH

A7
TO
EDINBURGH

ABBEY

HOSPITAL

TO
A7 CARLISLE

RIVER
EWES

RIVER ESK

THOMAS TELFORD BRIDGE

SUSPENSION
BRIDGE

PARK

STEPS

COTTAGE

·┼·┼·	ROUTE
	ROAD
	BRIDGE
∿∿∿	RIVER or STREAM
┼	GATE or STILE
xxxx	POWER LINE
	HEATHER or GRASSLAND
ᴑᴑᴑᴑᴑ	WALL

The walk begins in the car park adjacent to the A7 on the north side of the town. There is ample parking by the banks of the Ewes Water just before it joins the River Esk. Spare a few moments for the welcome visitors on the banks of the river – Mallard ducks. There are plenty of areas in which to picnic on the river bank or to watch the dippers and sand-pipers swooping along just above the rushing waters.

Begin the walk by going towards the town centre and turning sharp left up Drove Road and then forking left again, this time into Arkenholm Terrace. This will bring you to the golf course, from where a wide track, used by both pony and walker, leads halfway to the summit. The track has all the makings of an old drove road with dykes on either side. A few seats have been placed strategically for the weary traveller. On the left you will pass the public water supply for the town before reaching a gate and a stile to cross over into the open hill country.

From here, the track becomes much narrower as it winds its way through the heather and grassland. Keep an eye open for the numerous birds such as curlew and skylark that frequent those hills. The only blots on the landscape are the electricity pylons strung out like giant intruders; one wonders why those could not have been placed underground.

As well as the monument it bears, this hill is also famous for the Whita Well, believed to be the source of water for many illicit whisky stills.

Pass to the left of a pylon and then climb, gently at first, eventually more steeply, to the monument, guarded by a fence. There is a seat here and it is worthwhile, despite the pylons, to take time to admire the breathtaking scenery.

Don't forget, though, that the monument stands at 1,165 feet and it is likely to be much colder than in Langholm, so take some warm clothing.

Now retrace your steps down the track to the clubhouse of the golf club and go straight ahead down the road to reach the main street at the Eskdale Hotel. Cross over, slightly to the right, pass the hospital, and turn down Charles Street Old. This will bring you to the suspension bridge. It is noted that

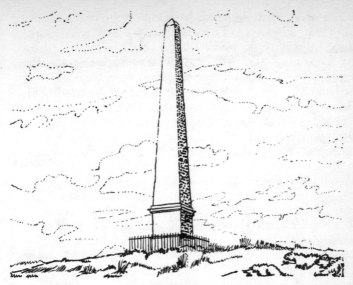

Malcolm Monument, in memory of a Governor of Bombay

the first bridge, built of wood in 1871, collapsed when large crowds gathered to take photographs of it.

Cross the bridge, go straight ahead for approximately 100 yards, and turn left over an iron bridge. At the end of this bridge, turn right onto a riverside path. Follow this past an old ford on the right for around 250 yards before turning sharp left uphill through thick woodland.

At the top of the hill you will reach a signpost indicating Warbla, Easton's Walk, and Gaskill's Walk. Take the track that goes straight ahead to Warbla, passing a cottage on the right, and head out into the land of the curlew and golden plover.

The path climbs up to the right passing woodland on the left to reach a gate and a stone stile. Continue ahead over the stile for 300 yards to reach a seat on the right of the track. Turn right and descend to the top of the wood that runs parallel with the route just followed. At the wood, turn right, go through a gate and a field to reach another gate, and then follow a track separating a field and the wood. This track will lead the walker back to the cottage. Turn left and go through the gate on the right, descending steps into the park and play area.

Return to the suspension bridge, but turn left before crossing and go along the road to the Thomas Telford bridge. Cross the water and turn left at the main street to return to the car park.

Walk 12
GRETNA GREEN
DUMFRIES & GALLOWAY
$4\frac{1}{2}$ miles

Gretna Green has become famous down the years for the many runaway marriages once conducted there. Young couples, barred by law from marrying south of the border, could, after spending two weeks of seclusion in Scotland, be married over the blacksmith's anvil without the consent of their parents.

English couples had to be 21 years of age before they could marry in their own country. But with Gretna only a few miles over the border north of Carlisle, it was comparatively easy for them to elope and be married there.

It was at Gretna Hall Hotel, built in 1710, that such 'marriages of declaration' took place, and, later, in the smithy. The young couple concerned required two witnesses, and when they returned to their own country their marriage was accepted as legal and binding.

Many youngsters were pursued over the border by their parents who would try to annul the marriages. Yet by law in Scotland these were legal and there was nothing the parents could do after the couple had had their marriage vows affirmed over the anvil. Quite often couples would arrive during the night and arouse the blacksmith from his bed requesting to be married. Without question he would perform the ceremony there and then, and the couple could return home as man and wife.

Marriages at Gretna go back as far as 1792. Over the years the famous anvil has been associated with thousands of

GRETNA GREEN

1 mile

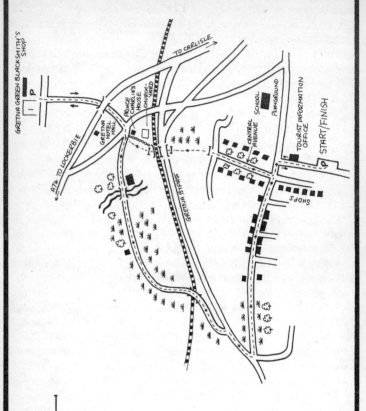

GRETNA GREEN BLACKSMITH'S SHOP

P

↑ TO CARLISLE

A74 TO LOCKERBIE

PRINCE CHARLIE'S HOUSE

CHURCH-YARD

GRETNA HOTEL HALL

GRETNA BYPASS

SCHOOL

PLAYGROUND

CENTRAL AVENUE

SHOPS

TOURIST INFORMATION OFFICE

P

START/FINISH

ROUTE	
ROAD	
BRIDGE	
GATE OR STILE	
RAILWAY	
FIELD + PASTURE LAND	
WALL	

marriages. One blacksmith by the name of Richard Rennison performed no fewer than 5,147 ceremonies. Although such marriages ceased to be legal in 1940, over a thousand couples still go each year to the register office in Gretna to be married – the appeal remains.

Today the old blacksmith's shop has been transformed into a visitors' centre, and to meet present time's commercial demand the Auld Smiddy restaurant has been opened next door to the centre.

Visitors to the centre today are greeted by a piper, and a favourite photograph is one taken by the anvil in a jocular wedding ceremony. The centre is open from March to September.

The walk begins in the village of Gretna, which is split by the main trunk A74 road from Glasgow to Carlisle and the Gretna by-pass. There is a car park about 50 yards from the Tourist Information Centre in the middle of the village. There are public bus services from Dumfries, Longtown, and Carlisle.

Turn right out of the car park and walk diagonally through a park with swings to reach the main road. Cross over the road and walk along the attractive, and graceful tree-lined Central Avenue, to another road. Cross this and go through a gate on the opposite side. Continue on the path that bisects the fields. At the opposite side of the field go under the Gretna by-pass and the railway, which runs from Carlisle to Glasgow via Dumfries and Kilmarnock, formerly part of the Caledonian Railway.

The coming of the railway had major implications for Gretna. In the beginning the Caledonian station was situated south of the border; later, Gretna Green became the first station on part of the Glasgow and South Western Railway to be served by a North British service from Longtown. Today, expresses pound their way through Gretna without stopping – a fact that would have been welcomed when the railway came to Gretna as there were complaints of this having resulted in a big increase in the number of marriages.

At the far end of the tunnel, go through another gate and

Gretna Green, famous for runaway marriages

follow the path that goes slightly right towards a cemetery. Go along beside the wall to reach another road. Cross this and take the road that goes virtually straight ahead. Pass under the A74 road, and after 100 yards you will reach the white-walled visitor centre and blacksmith's shop.

Take some time while at the centre to also see the coach museum which contains superb examples of coaches similar to those once used by elopers. You can also see a display of farm implements.

On leaving the centre, go back down the road under the A74 to reach the junction. Turn right, and then take the road that leads to the left. Continue on this road, passing on a gentle bend a farm on the right. You will soon cross over the railway before coming down to reach the by-pass. Take care while crossing this busy road.

Once across, go right for a few yards before turning left onto a quiet road that will bring you back into the centre of Gretna. The beginning of the Solway can easily be seen, while on a clear day the 3,000 foot mountain of Skiddaw in the Lake District dominates the distant skyline.

Walking back into Gretna one can appreciate the benefits

the by-pass has brought to the town – no more heavy juggernauts thundering through the centre. At the bottom of Central Avenue turn right and return to the car park.

Walk 13
CASTLE POINT
DUMFRIES & GALLOWAY
5 miles

Today the Solway Coast is best known for its sands and mudflats where the tides ebb and flow in dangerous mood; yet in days gone by holiday resorts such as Rockcliffe and Kippford enjoyed a different kind of fame, being havens for the smuggler. This walk explores the haunts of those smugglers as well as visiting much earlier sites.

The walk will take you from Kippford along the coast and cliffs to Castle Point, the site of an ancient fort dating from 400 BC, with magnificent views over the Solway. On a clear day, England's Lake District and Cumbrian towns of Maryport and Whitehaven can be seen, seemingly only an arm's distance away.

Set high up on a cliff with a sheer drop towards the sea, Castle Point marks the extremity of this walk, although it is possible to continue on the footpath as far as Sandyhills. However, this entails a rather unexciting return by road.

In comparison with Rockcliffe, Castle Point can be cold and windy, taking as it does the full brunt of the winds that sweep in from the sea. Nevertheless, it offers a superb vantage point.

The walk, part of which crosses land owned by the National Trust for Scotland, visits one of the most famous archaeological sites in southern Scotland at the Mote of Mark, given to the Trust by John and James McLellan in 1937 in memory of their brother, the late Col. William McLellan, and the grave of smuggler Joseph Nelson.

CASTLE POINT

N

1 mile

ROUTE
ROAD
BRIDGE
RIVER or STREAM
GATE or STILE
WALL
ROCKS AND CRAGS
GRASSLAND

START/FINISH

To DALBEATTIE A710

KIPPFORD

PHONE BOX

POST OFFICE

DALBEATTIE FOREST

MOTE OF MARK

HOTEL

ROCKCLIFFE

To COLVEND

FIELD

CASTLE POINT

ROUGH ISLAND

Kippford, the starting point of the walk, is served by public transport from Dalbeattie, and lies four miles south of that town. Motorists should take the A710 from Dalbeattie; Kippford is reached via a minor road to the right, and for the motorist there is parking at the entrance to the village next to the headquarters of the Solway Yacht Club.

From the car park, turn left into the village, and on reaching the post office turn left up the hill. The road then swings right to reach the Muckle Lands and Jubilee Path, five and a half acres of rough coastline. Here the tarred road ends and the path begins. This area, under the jurisdiction of the National Trust, offers splendid views over to Rough Island, which is a bird sanctuary. You are advised not to visit it in May or June when the birds are nesting. Also, make sure of the tides before attempting to visit the island at low water.

The path goes along the top of the headland; on the left is Mark Hill in the Dalbeattie Forest. A number of seats have been placed here, and it is worth stopping to admire the scenery, casting an eye to the village of Kippford.

The path winds its way through gorse and broom to reach the edge of the forest. On the right is the Mote of Mark, which you will visit on the return journey. Continue straight ahead along a narrow and pretty lane to reach the roadway at the top of Rockcliffe. Turn right down the hill, and at the shore turn left to follow the road along in front of some delightful homes.

Rockcliffe, like Kippford, is a haven for the visitor and wildlife enthusiast, for the coast is home to a wide variety of sea birds, from redshanks to oystercatchers.

After 250 yards, the walker will reach a road branching off to the right and marked 'The Merse'. This is a private road, but gives access to the footpath that leads to Castle Point.

Follow this road and join the footpath, marked by a sign, that leads off to the right. Go over a footbridge and continue on the path through more gorse and bushes. The path has been renovated by volunteers with support from the Countryside Commission for Scotland, the Scottish Rights of Way Society, and a number of private individuals.

Rockcliffe, a picturesque village on the Solway coast

The path continues close to the shore, and on approaching the last house actually goes down onto the sand and gravel beach. After passing the last house, the path swings round to reach the grave of Joseph Nelson, who came from Workington. He was drowned in a shipwreck in 1791; the stone was erected by his widow.

Continue on the path, cross over a stone stile, and follow the path round the edge of a field to reach a gate and the final climb to Castle Point. Here is a very informative indicator board identifying the surrounding landmarks.

Retrace your steps back to Rockcliffe. Turn left past the car park, cross the road, go through a narrow lane, and into the area known as the Mote of Mark. Go halfway across a field diagonally and then turn slightly left to cross a footbridge. Go straight ahead to reach a noticeboard at the foot of the Mote of Mark.

This site was excavated in 1913 and again in 1973. Fragments of baked clay moulds suggested a casting in metal of Celtic brooches, and pieces of glass of Mediterranean origin also suggested ninth-century occupation.

Turn left to go to the top of the Mote, and then descend by the path leading off from the right. This path continues slightly right, crossing other paths, to the edge of the forest once again. Turn left on the path followed earlier, go past two seats, and then take the track down to the left, through scrub and trees, to reach a wall. Go down between houses to reach the shoreline. Turn right and follow this road back to the car park.

Walk 14
THREAVE CASTLE
DUMFRIES & GALLOWAY
3 miles

Threave Castle, two and a half miles west of Castle Douglas in Dumfries and Galloway, is unique among similar bastions of strength in the south of Scotland as it stands on an island, small but picturesque, surrounded by the River Dee.

The castle celebrated a chequered career during numerous campaigns down the ages, often coming under siege but holding out against enemies of varying forces. It was a strong fortress and the remains standing today bear testament to the strength of its defences across the waters of the Dee.

The history of the surrounding area dates back to Roman times when there was a camp at Glenlochar, three miles further upstream on the Dee, but this is not visible except by aerial photographs. The history of the castle goes back to the fourteenth century. It was bought by Black Archibald the Grim, the third Earl of Douglas, who had been taken prisoner at the Battle of Poitiers in 1361. He succeeded as third Earl after the second died at Otterburn in 1388. He himself died at Threave Castle on Christmas Eve, 1400.

It was during the rebellion of the Black Douglases in 1455 that Threave Castle gained the fame for which it is best remembered today. The famous cannon Mons Meg, now in Edinburgh Castle, was summoned to do battle, and in the end the castle conceded to the enemy, but not without a magnificent fight. It is possible to see the holes in the castle's walls made by the cannon.

In the years that followed, the castle was granted in turn to

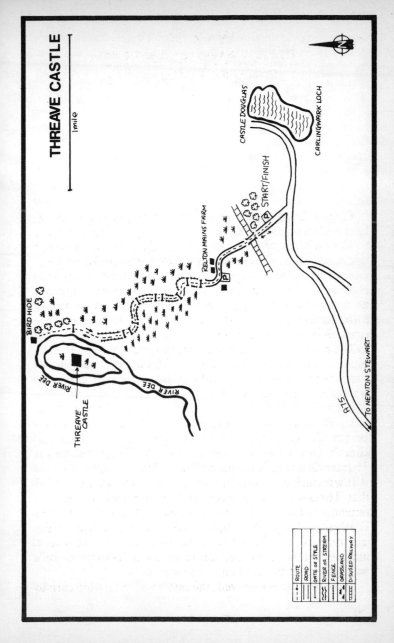

THREAVE CASTLE

1 mile

N

BIRD HIDE

THREAVE CASTLE

RIVER DEE

RIVER DEE

KELTON MAINS FARM

P

START/FINISH

CASTLE DOUGLAS

CARLINGWARK LOCH

A75

TO NEWTON STEWART

ROUTE
ROAD
GATE or STYLE
RIVER or STREAM
FENCE
GRASSLAND
DISUSED RAILWAY

Queen Margaret of Denmark, the Red Douglases, and eventually the Earl of Bothwell. In 1640 it came under attack from the Covenanters, and it held out for 13 weeks before the surrender was given. During the Napoleonic wars the castle accommodated French prisoners.

In view of its history, it is difficult to understand how the castle has managed to remain quite intact. It comes under the care of the Ancient Monuments Division of the Scottish Development Department, whose care and attention has kept history alive by the banks of the River Dee. Access to this fine castle is by a path leading from the A75 Euro route from Dumfries to Stranraer. There is a bell which the visitor must ring to draw the attention of the custodian, who will then ferry you across to the castle by rowing boat.

The walk begins on a farm road which leads from the A75 two miles south of Castle Douglas. Bus services to Stranraer pass on the main road, and there is parking at Kelton Mains Farm. For this walk, however, the car can be left just off the farm road 50 yards from the junction with the A75.

Turn right onto the farm road, and walk along this road to cross over the disused railway line which ran from Castle Douglas to Newtown Stewart. Continue on the road to reach Kelton Mains. The road turns left, where there is the official car park, and then leads to the path, which will take the walker to the castle.

Please keep to the path that passes through pleasant pastureland as you will be crossing over land where sheep will be grazing. There are also a number of gates which, of course, must be closed as necessary.

The top structure of the castle will soon appear in the distance, but after a mile you will be able to enjoy the full view of the castle. Continue on the path as it winds its way north-westwards to reach the banks of the river, until you reach the point from which to contact the custodian. The castle is only open during certain hours, and to make sure of going across to the island, it is advised to go there during the hours of opening. Telephone Castle Douglas 2611 for details.

After visiting the castle – and on a pleasant day a splendid

Threave Castle

afternoon can be enjoyed pottering around the small island – cross back to the 'mainland'. Turn left, cross a stile, and continue for 300 yards to reach a hut built as a hide for bird enthusiasts. It is worth spending some time here watching the wildlife on the river.

It is necessary to retrace the same route back to the start of the walk as the surrounding land is private.

Walk 15
ST NINIAN'S CAVE
DUMFRIES & GALLOWAY
3 miles

Although by necessity this is not a circular walk, it will take you back into the history of the early days of Christianity in southern Scotland. An additional bonus is that part of your route will take you through the delightful Physgill Glen.

Your objective on this walk is St Ninian's Cave, which pierces into the seashore rock on the south coast of an area lying west of Burrow Head known as the Machars. It is situated close to Port Castle Bay in one of several inlets protected by the high cliffs that dominate this jagged coast-line.

The peninsula whose rock houses the cave is a typical feature of the Solway coast south-west of the Isle of Whithorn. On this island, St Ninian's Chapel marks the spot at which the Christian pilgrims might possibly have arrived by sea. St Ninian was closely associated with early Christianity in the fifth century. Not a great deal is known about this mysterious missionary except that he did have associations with the south of Scotland – as witnessed by the cathedral priory at Whithorn, and the nearby chapel.

St Ninian's aim was to preach the gospel of Christianity to the inhabitants of this south-western corner. Although a monastery was created at Whithorn which became the focal point for Christians over the years, it was only in 1821 that an incised cross was found at the chapel thus establishing a link with St Ninian. In due course, other crosses were also found, and in 1884 there were major excavations at the cave. A major

ST NINIAN'S CAVE

1 mile

Legend:
- ROUTE
- ROAD
- BRIDGE
- GATE or STILE
- RIVER or STREAM
- FENCE
- GRASSLAND
- STONY SHORELINE

TO A747
ISLE OF WHITHORN -
STRANRAER ROAD

START/FINISH

SIGN

KIDSDALE FARM

GRASS HEADLAND

ST NINIAN'S CAVE

PORT CASTLE BAY

discovery was that of crosses cut in boulders as well as interesting pieces of stone. These were taken to the museum at Whithorn, well worth a visit.

Several crosses were discovered cut into the walls of the cave, and these are thought to have been engraved by pilgrims on their visits to these shores. Some of the crosses are believed to date back to the eighth century. There is no doubt in the minds of experts that St Ninian's Cave was a popular spot for pilgrims.

The cave comes under the auspices of the Ancient Monuments Division of the Scottish Development Department, and although it was once possible to enter the cave, it was found necessary to close it following a rockfall. At the time of writing it was not known whether it would be reopened or not in the future.

The starting point for the walk, near Physgill House, is reached by a minor road leading south from the A747 one mile east of that road's junction with the A746. There is no public transport to the starting point, though there are bus services to Whithorn, further inland. Drive to the car park near the farm of Kidsdale; the walk is signposted from there – a delightful ramble through the pretty woods of Physgill.

Go out of the car park and turn left. Walk towards the farm and take the narrow track down to the right that leads into the wood. Do not follow the road marked private. These are private woods and the walker is privileged to have access to the cave through them. Therefore, please make sure to keep to the path at all times.

Continue on the path to the spot where it divides over the stream that runs down from Ersock Loch to the sea. Take either track as they rejoin after a further 50 yards.

This narrow glade, laced with trees and bursting with daffodils in spring and autumnal plants later in the year, is a delightfully colourful approach to the coast. The trees which line the avenue hang gracefully overhead to provide a canopy through which the sun sparkles on a summer's day – truly a world apart from everyday bustle. Continue on the path to reach a gate, at which the line of trees stops.

St Ninian's Cave, focal point for early Christians

Go straight ahead on the track that is now grassy; the waves of the Atlantic will be seen breaking gently on the Solway coastline. The path is still hemmed in, but gradually it opens out as you near the shoreline. Turn right on the 'beach', which is well endowed with stone. Look straight ahead and you will see the cave of St Ninian standing beneath the distant headland.

Walk along the shore to reach the approach to the cave – there is a track on the right round the huge boulders. Take care if the rocks are wet after rain or soaked by spray from the sea.

The cave is set back into the rock. An information board gives a brief history of the site, telling the visitor that in 1950 it was confirmed as having a long history of occupation dating back to at least the eighth century and that inside the walls have been inscribed by the pilgrims.

Take time to view the coastline from the cave before returning to the car park by the same route.

Walk 16
BRUCE'S STONE
DUMFRIES & GALLOWAY
5 miles

Bruce's Stone is a large boulder of rock perched high on a plinth on ground at the head of Loch Trool. It was erected overlooking, on the opposite side of the loch, the site of the skirmish in 1307 which marked the opening of the campaign of independence that led to King Robert the Bruce's success over King Edward at Bannockburn in 1314.

The memorial was erected 600 years after the death of Bruce – it was unveiled in June, 1929, with an inscription on the stone telling its story.

The walk encompasses in part a route set out by the Forestry Commission, who have succeeded in marrying their needs with that of the visitor. It begins at the Caldons camp site, set in the middle of the glen, and will take the walker along the south side of the loch to return on a farm track and then a road on the northern flanks. For those interested in forestry it is a walk with special interest, and all will enjoy the rugged grandeur of the high peaks.

There are several other important sites to visit during the walk, and these will give the walker fine and extensive views down Glen Trool from both sides of the loch.

The Caldons camp site, at which the walk starts, is reached by a minor road to the right of the A714 eight miles north of Newton Stewart. There is no public transport. Here, in stark contrast to the afforested valley, soar the great hills – the highest, Merrick, rising to 2,766 feet, higher than any other in southern Scotland.

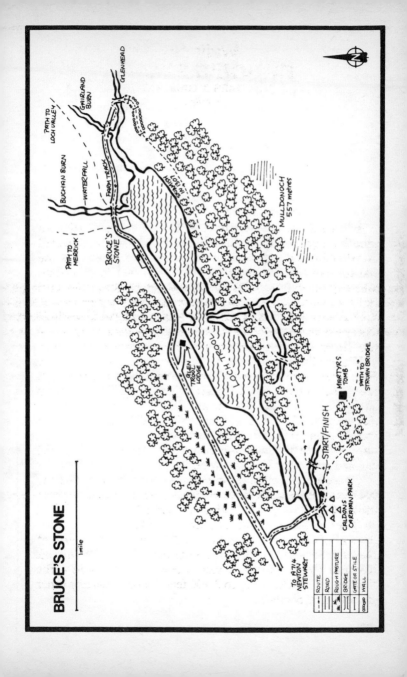

BRUCE'S STONE

1 mile

| ROUTE |
| ROAD |
| ROUGH PASTURE |
| BRIDGE |
| GATE OR STILE |
| WALL |

TO A714
NEWTON STEWART

CALDONS
CAIRYMAN PARK

START/FINISH

GLEN TROOL LODGE

LOCH TROOL

MARTYR'S TOMB

PATH TO
STRURN BRIDGE

LOCH IN
MULLDONCH
557 metres

BRUCE'S STONE

FARM TRACK

PATH TO MERRICK

PATH TO
LOCH VALLEY

BUCHAN BURN

WATERFALL

GAIRLAND
BURN

GLENHEAD

Cross over a bridge which spans the Caldons Burn, and go into the camp site. It is worth diverting to visit the Martyrs' tomb. After 100 yards, take the path on the right; follow this for 200 yards through the woodland to reach the tomb.

It was here that six martyrs – James and Robert Duns, Thomas and John Stevenson, Andrew McCall and James McClive – perished in the cause of Covenanting, the bond entered into by Scottish Presbyterians to defend their religion. They met regularly at the Caldons site and the memorial was erected there by voluntary contributions. The original stone was damaged, and in 1983 it was transferred to the museum at Newton Stewart.

Return to the camp site and follow the path marked 'Forestry trail'. Go through the caravan park, keeping the Caldons House on the right, to enter the woodland at the end of the park. You will then follow a well-defined track through Scots Pine, European larch, and ash, birch, and rowan. In wet weather the track can be soft underneath.

The path is rough in places, climbing steeply for short distances as it edges its way along the side of the hill below Mulldonoch – 1,827 feet. Although the path zigzags as it meanders through the forest, the number of signs ensures that you will be able to follow the route.

Views are very restricted due to thick woodland, but it is possible to view the loch below at intervals through firebreaks or where the commission has opened up a clearing.

Continue on the path beyond the head of the loch before descending gradually. Cross over a stile, continue on the path for a further 300 yards, and then turn left down the side of a wood. Go over two stiles to reach a pleasant meadow near Glenhead. Cross the Glenhead Burn by a wooden bridge. This is a pleasant area in which to stop and have a short break or a picnic.

Turn left and follow the banks of the stream before turning right to cross an open field diagonally to join the farm track which leads to the road and then Bruce's Stone. Cross over the Gairland Burn and you will soon notice a track that leads to Loch Valley, Loch Neldricken, and Loch Enoch. Here,

Bruce's Stone, start of the campaign for independence

too, is the Buchan Burn, with its deep gully and the waters pounding over rocky outcrops. Take time to walk up the right-hand side of the burn for 200 yards to admire some spectacular waterfalls.

Return to the road and turn right to follow it to Bruce's Stone, which commands a seemingly impregnable position dominating Loch Trool. Near here, a path leads off to Benyellary and Merrick. Go down from the stone and pass a craft shop to reach the car park. Follow the road for approximately one and a half miles before turning left at the road leading to the Caldons and back to the camp site.

Walk 17
CULZEAN CASTLE & COUNTRY PARK
STRATHCLYDE
6 miles

Culzean Castle and its surrounding country park consti-
tute what estate agents would undoubtedly term a prize site.
There can surely be a no more superlative position than
where it stands on the banks of the Firth of Clyde, looking
across to the beautiful island of Arran, and in the distance, on
a clear day, the coastline of Ireland.

Culzean is a large feather in Ayrshire's cap, and one has to
acknowledge the prominent part it plays in that county's
economy and, in a broader context, in Scotland's heritage.
The castle and country park draw around 300,000 visitors
each year – very much a Scottish jewel. It is owned by the
National Trust for Scotland, who made the acquisition in
1945. Since then the castle and the estate have been restored,
offering the visitor the opportunity to see one of the country's
grandest heirlooms.

At one time the estate and castle belonged to the Marquis
of Ailsa, but the castle is probably now most famous for the
guest flat which became a home for the former American
president Dwight D. Eisenhower. This has helped to forge
strong links between Culzean and the United States, and
Americans flock here in their thousands each year.
Eisenhower first visited Culzean in 1946. Less than a year
before, the National Trust had launched an appeal which
raised £20,000 in six months – a major effort forty years ago.

The castle was opened to the public in 1947. In the first
year visitors totalled 6,000; two years later this had jumped to

CULZEAN CASTLE & COUNTRY PARK

1 mile

N

Legend:
- ROUTE
- ROAD
- BRIDGE
- GATE OR STILE
- GRASS + SHRUBLAND

EXHIBITION CENTRE

CULZEAN CASTLE

TO AYR

STEPS

FIRTH OF CLYDE

SWAN LAKE

AVIARY

STEPS

PICNIC AREA

CARAVAN SITE

HOTEL

DISUSED RAILWAY TRACK

MAIDENS

START/FINISH

almost 50,000. Culzean was soon to climb to the top of the popularity poll, having branched out to encompass something for all the family.

Today Culzean offers a breathtakingly beautiful country park allied with a rugged coastline and the freedom to roam around its many attractions. The castle is open from Easter to October and the grounds are open all year round.

There are ample parking areas at Culzean within the grounds. Bus services from Ayr to Turnberry and Girvan pass the main entrance. But this walk begins in the picturesque village of Maidens, south of Culzean, from where the massive rock of Ailsa Craig can be seen standing dominantly in the Clyde. Drive into Maidens on the A719 from Ayr and turn right by the shore to a parking area facing the Firth of Clyde.

Leave the car park and continue on the narrow road which fronts the narrow beach in a north-easterly direction. Ignore the first road leading off to the left, and continue to the next junction where there is an old building. Turn left and go straight ahead to pass a small hotel on the left and then bear right to reach a caravan park.

Follow the path through the caravan park to enter the woods of Culzean by going over a stile. Continue straight ahead until you reach a car park on the left. Take the path that leads off to the left to pass the aviary and continue until you reach Swan Lake. This lives up to the name with swans among its inhabitants, together with various species of duck and herons.

Turn right and walk along the side of the lake before entering thick woodland, following the track which meanders through the rhododendrons and along the top of the cliffs, to emerge into open parkland just beyond the private residence of Dolphin House.

The magnificent splendour of Culzean Castle now strikes you full on. Go ahead over the parkland in a diagonal direction, through a gate, to emerge at the Orange conservatory. Lack of funds have so far prevented the conservatory from being renovated.

Culzean Castle, where American president Dwight D. Eisenhower had a room

Go left up the steps to reach the castle and continue straight ahead to reach the entrance. Beyond the entrance is an indicator viewpoint, with a magnificent panorama of the Firth of Clyde mirrored superbly in the blue waters rushing against the rocky coastline.

When you leave the castle, follow the path signposted to the Park Centre, formerly the Home Farm, now accommodating an exhibition area – including videos which depict the history of Culzean – a restaurant, and a gift shop.

One can spend a whole day at Culzean, exploring the numerous paths and avenues. Follow the roadway now that leads to the former light railway between Alloway Junction and Turnberry. It was opened in 1906, and although closed in 1931, it was re-opened a year later, but for only 11 months. The Maidens and Dunure Railway, built mainly to serve Turnberry golf course, was never a success. Part of the route has now been converted into a walkway.

At the rail bridge descend the steps on the left to the old

track and turn left. Pass over two bridges and continue, to go under a third bridge. After approximately 300 yards the track becomes more overgrown, and where the track peters out go down to the left and over a stile. Turn right and go down the road to reach the old building passed earlier in the walk. Turn left and walk back to your car.

Walk 18
ROBERT BURNS' COTTAGE
STRATHCLYDE
3 miles

Robert Burns, arguably the greatest poet Scotland has ever produced, was born in the village of Alloway, south of Ayr, on January 25th, 1759. His reputation and fame is international and each year around the end of the month of January the poet is remembered in Burns' suppers from Edinburgh to Moscow, London to Brisbane.

It was a tough upbringing for the young Burns. He was a ploughman and gained a great deal of his inspiration from long days spent toiling in the fields. He loved the simple things in life: all the facets of nature and the countryside in which he lived. He also loved the girls – the lassies.

His poetry reflected the basic simplicity of the land he worked to make a living, and the simple lives of the people he knew. Perhaps his greatest poem was 'Tam O'Shanter', a tale of witches and warlocks who, disturbed when Tam was going home one night in a drunken state, chased him from their revelry in the church.

Ayrshire is Burns country. There is now a Burns' Trail, which the motorist can follow to visit all the famous haunts of Scotland's national bard, perhaps an even greater figure than William Wallace, Robert the Bruce, or Bonnie Prince Charlie.

Burns was the son of a tenant farmer, William Burns, and he was born and spent the first seven years of his life in the cottage, or 'auld clay biggin', which had been built by his father and which is the objective of this walk. The cottage

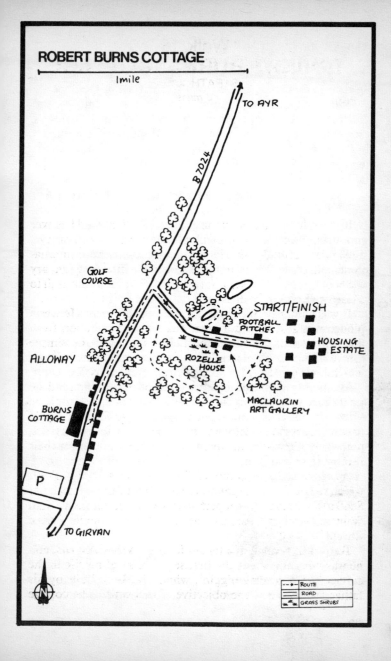

stands alongside the B7024 road from Ayr.

The cottage is preserved as a museum and many relics of the time of the poet are on display. It now attracts thousands of visitors each year and is open from April to October.

Other famous Burns' landmarks in the near vicinity are the Old Bridge of Doon, marking the end of Tam O'Shanter's escape from the witches; the Burns' Monument, completed in 1823; in the gardens, the life-size statues of Tam O'Shanter and his drinking companion Souter Johnnie; and the haunted Alloway Kirk.

If you are using public transport, take the bus from Ayr which passes the front door of the cottage and start the walk from there. Motorists should drive into Rozelle Park by taking the minor road which runs off to the east from the B7024 just over half a mile north of the cottage. You can park about half a mile along this road close to Rozelle House on the right.

The walk through the park is delightful for its flower beds are seas of colour throughout most of the year. Rhododendrons and numerous colourful shrubs lend grace and charming elegance to the parkland, while the ponds are busy with ducks and other wildlife. Rozelle Park encompasses nearly a hundred acres of woodland, presented to the people of Ayr by Hamilton's descendants in 1968. The park is famed for its rare trees, including Lebanon cedars and American redwood, but its abundance of flowers also attracts many visitors. In spring it is worth making a visit just to see the glorious azaleas which brighten up even a dull day – or the thousands of daffodils adding dashes of yellow in almost every corner.

Rozelle House was built in the 1750s by Robert Hamilton, an Ayrshire man who made his fortune in Jamaica. The house took its name from one of Hamilton's many properties in the Caribbean.

To start the walk, go along the road, past the house and the adjacent art gallery, to reach a number of football pitches. At the end of the roadway, at the entrance to a housing estate, turn right to follow a path through woodland adjacent to the

Burns' Cottage, birthplace of the famous Scottish poet

pitches. A bridle path, protected by a fence, comes in from the left. Keep on the path as it curves to the right through the estate until you emerge close to the entrance to the park.

Turn left to leave the park and left again on the main road. Follow this to Burns' Cottage, a typical stone and clay farm building with a thatched roof.

After visiting the cottage, retrace your route along the main road – with the famous Ayr Belleisle golf course on your left – to re-enter Rozelle Park. Continue along the roadway until you reach a pond on the left; here, take the track that leads beside the two ponds and follow this round them. There are a number of seats – ideal places to sit and quietly observe the beautiful surroundings, tucked away from the main road only a few hundred yards away.

Return to the park road for the short walk back to your starting point.